YOUR KNOWLEDGE HAS VALUE

Godlove Lawrent

The Rationale of Studying Comparative Education to Students in Tanzanian Educational Institutions

Challenges and Implications for the Future

GRIN Publishing

Bibliographic information published by the German National Library:

The German National Library lists this publication in the National Bibliography; detailed bibliographic data are available on the Internet at http://dnb.dnb.de .

Imprint:

Copyright © 2012 GRIN Verlag, Open Publishing GmbH
Print and binding: Books on Demand GmbH, Norderstedt Germany
ISBN: 978-3-656-16238-4

This book at GRIN:

http://www.grin.com/en/e-book/191430/the-rationale-of-studying-comparative-education-to-students-in-tanzanian

GRIN - Your knowledge has value

Since its foundation in 1998, GRIN has specialized in publishing academic texts by students, college teachers and other academics as e-book and printed book. The website www.grin.com is an ideal platform for presenting term papers, final papers, scientific essays, dissertations and specialist books.

Visit us on the internet:

http://www.grin.com/

http://www.facebook.com/grincom

http://www.twitter.com/grin_com

The Rationale of Studying Comparative Education to Students in Tanzanian Educational

Institutions: Challenges and Implications for the Future.

Mr. Godlove Lawrent

Abstract

This paper gives the critical justifications for studying comparative education to students in educational institutions in Tanzania. It also tries to trace back the short historical perspectives of the field of comparative education, challenges facing the field of comparative education in Tanzania and the implications of the field of comparative education for future improvement of the educational systems. The paper concludes that, the study of comparative education is very important for all Tanzanian students as it enables them become good educational policy makers, educational planners and educational analysts. This paper also insists that the study of comparative education is essential for adoption of policies useful for improving the education quality in the country. However this paper suggests that there is a need to make the study of comparative education as a compulsory discipline to all students from primary to tertiary level.

Introduction

Historically, the field of comparative education grew from international Education which analyzes and fosters international orientation in knowledge and attitudes and brings together students, teachers and scholars from different nations to learn about and from each other (BAICES, 1973). However, comparative education itself refers to the study of various and often contrasting educational systems with a view of understanding the similarities and differences (University of Nairobi, 1993). It studies why educational systems (structure, organization, curricula and financing) and processes vary, and how education relates to wider social factors and forces. Likewise, BAICES (1973) defines comparative education as an academic and interdisciplinary subject which applies historical, philosophical and social science theories and methods to classify and explain characteristics of different nations' educational system. The study has long based its insights on number of countries and case studies of national education systems.

Before 1950s, the study focused mainly on philosophical and cultural origins of national educational system (Carnoy and Rhoten, 2002). Today, the field of comparative education is moving towards more sophisticated examination in relation to economic, political and social forces (Arnove, 2008). Furthermore, Adick (1992) claims that, comparative education focuses much on explaining the diversity of development, processes of expansion and systematization of modern education in different countries. Bray (2007) emphasizes that, comparative educators are interested in examining the similarities and differences in the educational processes of various groups, the examination of the educational relationships obtained between the developed and developing areas.

Rationale of Studying Comparative Education

In actual fact, students in educational institutions are not prepared without the study of comparative education due to the following justifiable reasons. Comparative education provides reference for reforms. Through studying the educational systems of other countries we can discover which reforms are possible and desirable (University of Nairobi, 1993). In the 1990s, for example before adopting educational reforms for grade 7 and 8; China studied the reforms in Australia, England, Sweden, New Zealand and United States (Joong, et al, 2009). Before the reform, the Chinese educational curriculum demanded students to study the same material, memorizing text and writing examination. Therefore, China used the experience from those countries to implement the reform. In the same way, Argentina learned to Chile the decentralization reforms of Education and hence, adopted (Narodowski and Nores, 2001).

Through this reference, it is essentially important for Tanzanian students to study comparative education for the same purposes. It is clear from this lesson that the education reforms in Tanzania follow the similar path.

The study helps students to improve the education in their home country. Comparative education helps students to acquire better understanding of education system of other countries and borrow some aspects for better improvement of education at home. Paige (2005) emphasizes that, comparative education contributes to the internalization of school curriculum and student learning experience, develop students' broader world views, cross–cultural and comparative analytical skills. Similarly, the study of comparative education helps students to make connection between the local and global, and the relationship between education, development and society.

Furthermore, comparative education help students to understand how educational systems are shaped by wealth, ideology, social cultural features of the country and impacts of globalization on education policy and practice in different regions and countries (Padavil, 2009). Narodowski and Nores (2001) maintain that, the last decades were largely characterized by the amount of content of the education policies developed worldwide due to the downfall of the USSR. Therefore educational policies in Latin America and other continents were dramatically altered to reflect changed economic policies. The Tanzania Education system is shaped by the ideology of socialism and self-reliance, thus all educational polices reflect the philosophy of education for self-reliance. Carnoy and Rhoten (2002) claim that, globalization is a force reorganizing the world's economy and the main resources for that economy are increasing knowledge and information. The global economy in turn shapes the nature of educational opportunities and institutions, thus, studying comparative education is very essential since it helps students in Tanzania and the world as whole to understand how economic, social cultural and ideological factors affect the education system in a particular nation/country.

This field of comparative education is also helpful in the whole process of preparing educational leaders who can act effectively and ethically within the structure, process and cultural content of organized education, who will serve in education leadership roles of the country and the world as administrator, scholars and educational-related policy analysts, who will provide mission-related services and who will proved leadership in the solution of current problems in Education (Paige, 2005). Marginson and Mollis (2001) insist that, comparative education from time to time produce insights and techniques that open doorway for government and educational management. Therefore, comparative education should be taught to all students in the field of education in Tanzania in order to make them become good educational analysts and policy makers.

It also helps students to increase an understanding about the process of donating and receiving knowledge, acquiring, reconciling and maximizing it in the interest of both donors and recipients. Through studying comparative education, students can understand how some countries donate and receive knowledge for the benefit of the nation and donors themselves (University of Nairobi, 1993). Arnove (2008) asserts that, most of the former colonies have dramatically expanded their education by involving substantial amounts of external technical assistance (money, equipment's and personnel) and they have sent many people abroad to receive advanced training, hence to him this is one kind of neo-colonialism. In some countries like Tanzania, the provision of education for secondary and tertiary level is through cost sharing while in some countries educational provision is free of charge. In Netherlands for instance, all schooling up to secondary level is compulsory and free (Galabawa et al, 2007). It is important to note that cost sharing policy in most developing countries particularly Tanzania was greatly influenced by the Structural Adjustment Policy in the early 1990s as a condition for the country to be accessible to education related loans and grants.

Through this study, students can be in the position to know other people, particularly educators and scholars who contributed to the development of the field of comparative education. The influential scholars in this field are as Brian Holmes who wrote a book "Problems in a comparative approach" in 1995, Edmund King who wrote a book "Other schools and ours: Comparative studies for Today in 1970. Other scholars who contributed a lot in this field are as Nicholas Hans (famous scholar in comparative Education at the University of London), Harold Noah and Eckstein Max wrote a book "Towards science of comparative Education" while Barber wrote an article called "science, salience and comparative education" (Marginson & Mollis, 2001).Bray et al (2007) argue that, most people see comparative education as a field which welcome scholars who are equipped with tools from other arenas but who choose to focus on educational issues in a comparative context.

Comparative education makes students practical, realistic, appreciate and acknowledge other. Through studying comparative education an individual may improve his / her own system of education without fear. In order to improve the system of education we should learn what other countries do, acknowledge and appreciate them. China appreciated and acknowledged the reforms done in Australia, Sweden, New Zealand and United States and hence adopted the reform (Joong, 2009). Sadler as cited from Bray et al (2007) suggest that learning more about others culture and societies and then comparing patterns might encourage appreciation of domestic education system as well as heightening awareness of shortcomings. Comparative education can hold up a mirror for any nation to see its own school system more clearly and wisely (Edman, 1959). By studying comparative education, students can practice the experience learned from other countries. For example, comparative education research in the history of education has aroused the interest of an increasing number of Portuguese researchers (Madeira, 2006).

Nevertheless, the study of comparative education makes use of many types of learning other than textbook study since it encourages travel and learning of foreign languages, it spurs the creation and the useful functioning of all sorts of international professional organization and the publication of reports and periodicals. It also encourages good use of all sorts of exchange programmes and students (Edman, 1959). By studying comparative education, students can understand the quality of education provided in a particular country, and institutions can understand one another, therefore, exchange programmes, and students can also be possible. Some universities in Tanzania for example have an exchange programmes for their students with other universities elsewhere in the world. Such culture has an impact to students themselves and the country where these students are coming from. Through this programmes, students can be in the position to make the comparison of education systems of their countries in terms of structure, curricula, organization, financing and the like. These students are likely to have an influence to policy makers upon the return back to their home countries. However, this is only possible to countries with listening culture from educational stakeholders.

Students need to be acquainted with comparative Education skills for educational planning. This involves planning for curriculum, material selection and design, arranging the educational contexts and planning on the use of good methods of teaching and learning (Kandir et al, 2009). Planning here also includes enrolment expansions, teacher recruitment, construction of classrooms and provision of in-service teacher training (Galabawa et al, 2007). Comparative education helps students to learn how various countries plan for expansion of their educational systems in order to provide education for all citizens (University of Nairobi, 1993). Despite the fact that the policy formulation and implementation are as the results of international agendas, the adoption of the two comprehensive educational plans namely; the Primary Education Development Plan (PEDP) and Secondary Education Development Plan (SEDP) were adopted as a result of studying the achievement of the education sector of other countries which were doing the same (URT, 2004; Ndabise, 2008). The two have adopted with an attempt to increase expansion of education systems in primary and secondary education respectively.

Likewise, the study helps students and educators in problem solving. Bray, et al (2007) assert that, comparative education field promotes interdisciplinary collaboration in the development of comparative approaches to the study of educational problems and improve the exchange of information about research and methodological development in comparative education. Through studying the educational systems of other countries, students and others educators can be in the position to find the solution to educational related problems. Nichollis (2006) asserts that, the major focus of comparative education is to provide solutions of educational problems within a given school system or national contexts. Interdisciplinary interaction and collaboration draw attentions to students and educationists to learn from one another. In fact, there are common problems of educations, but some problems are unique. Therefore, the solution of such problems

7

can be solved by involving people with different expertise. This can only be accomplished through the study of the comparative education. For example, through studying comparative education as a discipline, one can be able learn from other countries how the issue of drop out was addressed for the sake the sake of adopting the same.

Challenges facing the study of comparative Education and Implication for the Future

The field of comparative education faces a lot of challenges. One among them is common language problems. Some writers and scholars of comparative education report or write articles and books using their home country language. For instance, comparative education in Chinese speaking communities is reported in Chinese, while other important comparative education is being reported in Japanese, Korean, Portuguese and various other languages (Bray, 2002). These languages are not familiar to the majority students in schools. This brings some problems to Tanzanian readers as they fail to interpret these foreign languages and adopt some policies for educational quality improvement. However, English language is commonly used in reporting most of the comparative education work (Wu and Hsieh, 2008). It is, thus, important to have language experts who can translate the comparative education-related literatures though the issue itself is cost effective.

Moreover, specialists in this field of comparative education are very few, this is due to the fact that, there is no special Masters degree on comparative and international education in Tanzania. Comparative education at Masters of education level is taught as a course, but not as a separate degree programme. However, in some universities in Tanzania this is treated as an optional course. This state of affairs makes students less familiar with the education systems of even their neighbor counterpart countries. In the developed countries, like in the United Kingdom various universities like the University of Newcastle and Sussex offer the masters degree in comparative education and development and comparative and international education respectively. This situation provides the chance to policy makers on what to adopt and what does not. In order to get many specialists in this field, it is recommended that, the course should be core to all students pursuing various degrees in education. Also academicians are encouraged to conduct various researches pertaining this field. This will enable them become competent and confident in the field. Once this is implemented, it is possible to have experts and competent policy makers in the field of comparative education.

Reference books and other comparative education related materials are still problem. There are very few books reporting the study of this field in Tanzanian academic institutions. Likewise, most of Tanzanian Libraries have very few references regarding to the study of this field. This is attributed to the fact that the field of comparative education is very young in Tanzanian context. Most of the content taught in Tanzanian institutions focuses on the local environment. Little is done in learning about the education of other countries. Therefore, great initiatives should be taken by the government to encourage the study of comparative education from primary to tertiary level. By doing so, it is possible for the country to get good educational policy analysts and educational policy makers for better education provision and improvement as whole. Similarly, various endeavors should be made to ensure that educational institutions are stocked with enough and relevant books on the field of comparative education.

The impact of intensified globalization is also a probably most important challenge in this field. Crossley (2002) explains that interest in globalization has attracted many new scholars and professionals to comparative and internal research, but at the same time, it has generated critiques of traditionally accepted modes of operation and frameworks of analysis. Due to the fact that the world is like a village, understanding and learning the education system of other countries is crucial. However, attention is needed is selecting what to adopt and what does not. Policy makers in this manner should adopt things which are relevant to the Tanzanian context without taking much attention on things which can not deteriorate the indigenous culture. In due course, good things should be taken and integrated to our curriculum while leaving the unwanted ones aside.

Conclusion

Generally the study of comparative education is very important not only to all students in educational institutions in Tanzania. This is due to the fact that it enables students become good educational policy makers, educational planners and educational analysts in the future. We cannot make any educational progress in our own country without studying and making comparison on the education of other countries. In educational arena, there is no country which is satisfactory for each and every thing. We depend from each other. This statement comply with Semali (1997) contention that "one white ant does not build an ant hill". The contention implies that in order to achieve the educational objectives we need to learn the systems of education from each other. In due course, comparative education should be made as a compulsory discipline to all students and it should be made a compulsory course for all students pursuing Bachelor degrees in Education rather than being an optional course. Higher learning institutions should have to think on the possibility to establish masters' degree on comparative education so as to get many educational planners and policy makers for the educational development of the country. However, we should advice educators to carry out various researches related to the field of comparative Education so as to get as many references as possible for the future education generation as Adick (1992) maintains that, education system is supposed to be designed for helping younger generations actualize their values and ideas.

References

Adick,C.(1992).Modern Education in Non-Western Societies in the Light of the world system Approach in Comparative Education, *International Review of Education*, 38(3), 241-255

Arnove,R.(1980). Comparative Education and World systems Analysis, *Comparative Education Review*,24(1), 48-62 retrieved in December 22,2009, from http://www.jstor.org/journals/ucpress.html

Bray, M.(2002). Comparative Education in East Asia: Growth, Development and Contribution of the field. *Current issues in Comparative Education,* 4(2), 70-79

Bray, M. (2007).Comparative Education Research: Approaches and Methods Hong Kong, Comparative Education Research Centre

British Association for International and Comparative Education Society (1973).*Journal of the Comparative Education Society in Europe*, 3(2), 8-13

Carnoy,M and Rhoten,D.(2002). What Does Globalization Mean for Education Change? A Comparative Approach. *Comparative Education Review*, 46(1), 1-9

Crossley, M. (2002).Comparative and International Education: Contemporary challenges, Reconceptualization and New Directions for the field. *Current issues in Comparative Education*, 4(2), 81-86

Edman,M.(1959). *Comparative Education: Professional Grapenuts?* Michigan. Wayne State University

Galabawa,J,C.et al.(2007). Papers in Education and Development, *Journal of the faculty of Education,* University of Dar-es Salaam, PED No.27

Joong, L.(2009).Investigation into the perceptions of students, parents and teacher in China's Education Reform in Grades 7and 8. *International Electronic Journal of Elementary Education,* 1(3), 142-154

Kandir,A.,Ozbey,S and Inal,G (2009). A study on the difficulties faced by preschool teachers in the planning and implementation. *The Journal of International Social Research,* 2(6), 374-386

Madeira,A.(2006). Comparative Studies in the History of Colonial Education: Consideration on Comparison in the Lusophone Space. *Educational Sciences Journal,* 1(1), 37-56. Retrieved in December,23, 2009 from http://www.sisifo.fpce.ul.pt

Marginson,S and Mollis,M.(2001)."*The door opens and the tiger leaps": Theories and Reflexivities of Comparative Education for a global millennium,* University of Buenos Aires

Narodowski,M & Nores, M.(2001).Socio-economic segregation with(without) Competitive Education Policies. A comparative analysis of Argentina and Chile. *Journal of Education policy,* 3 (2), 1-30

Ndabise, D. (2008). National Education Debate: Community Secondary School; How Long is their Journey to Quality Education. Paper presented at National Maktaba Conference Hall on 21 October 2008

Nichollis,J.(2006).From antithesis to Synthesis:Reinterpreting the Brian Holmes/Edmund King dialectic. *Research in Comparative and International Education,* 1 (4), 320-334

Padavil,G.(2009). *Foundations of Comparative Multicultural Education, Cross cultural Analysis of multicultural Education in the United States and selected areas of the world.* Illinois State University

Paige,M.(2005). Comparative and International Development Education *49th Annual Conference of Comparative and International Education Society.* Stanford University

University of Nairobi (1993).*Comparative Education.* Nairobi: University of Nairobi

URT (2004). Secondary Education Development Plan 2004-2005. Dar-es Salaam: MOEC

Wu, M,. and Hsieh,S,W.(2008).The comparison of oral Language acquisition for grade 1-3 in Taiwan and America, *International journal of Instruction,* 1(2), 1-24, retrieved on December 24,2009 from http://www.e-iji.net